# If You Are Suddenly Single

A helpful guide for widows on
how to handle your finances after
the death of your spouse

Brad Ledwith, CFP®

ISBN: 978-1-4834-7152-5 (sc)
ISBN: 978-1-4834-6879-2 (e)

Because of the dynamic nature of the Internet, any web addresses or links contained in this book may have changed since publication and may no longer be valid. The views expressed in this work are solely those of the author and do not necessarily reflect the views of the publisher, and the publisher hereby disclaims any responsibility for them.

Any people depicted in stock imagery provided by Thinkstock are models, and such images are being used for illustrative purposes only.
Certain stock imagery © Thinkstock.

Lulu Publishing Services rev. date: 06/06/2017

*This book is dedicated with love to my mom, Cindy.*

# Table of Contents

# Introduction

## Brad's story

I'll never forget the day I got the call that changed my life forever. I was sixteen years old and working at my summer job doing data transcription for a physical therapy clinic. When they told me my mom was calling, I knew something was wrong. She never called me at work. My stomach hurt as I walked the three feet to pick up the phone. The pain got worse when I heard her say, "You need to come home right away."

I raced home to find a crowd of people at my house—family, friends and neighbors. When I walked in the door, a friend of my mom's told me that my dad was gone. He had died unexpectedly while he was away on a business trip and had been found in his hotel room. That day my mom's life was turned upside down—and our lives along with hers.

In addition to the emotional shock, our lives were thrown into turmoil because of our new financial situation. My dad had just started a new job where he was making 100 percent commission. He had no life insurance and no real assets, and he had two children, one of them bound for college in another year.

At the time, my mom was working as a bank manager for the local branch of a national bank. Her salary was not going to be enough to pay the credit cards, the mortgage, the property taxes, and all the other expenses—not to mention sending my sister and me to college.

In the months and years after my dad died, I watched my mom struggle through the aftermath of his death. I saw the effect on her as she tried to grasp her financial situation and develop a plan for our future at the same time that she was grieving. The overwhelming emotions she was experiencing made it very hard for her to focus. To make matters worse, not having a financial plan in place also hampered her ability to make sound decisions. Even though my mom worked in a bank and had handled the day-to-day household finances, she still wasn't equipped to make the big financial decisions she now faced. And suddenly, after twenty-five years together, she no longer had my dad to bounce ideas off of and to help make those major decisions.

From seeing my mom go through this experience, and living through it with her, I developed a strong desire to help other surviving spouses get through the financial challenges of finding themselves suddenly single. This desire contributed to my decision to enter the financial field, engaging in a profession where I could help people who are going through the same situation.

## Who this book is for

This book is intended for women who have lost a spouse. In my years as a financial planner, I have worked with many recent widows. Most of them had been in what many consider a more traditional type of relationship, where the man takes care of the money and the woman takes care of the children and the household. In most cases, the husband was the major breadwinner and the one who handled the finances.

Even a woman who has participated in managing the family's finances in the past, however, will go through a period of emotional turmoil after losing her spouse, especially if the death was sudden, and this can make it difficult to handle the financial challenges that usually arise.

Although my clients' specific situations have varied, some universal themes run through their experiences. It is my hope that sharing what I've learned by going with my clients through their journeys will help you navigate through this difficult time as well.

## What you can expect from this book

If you are a surviving spouse reading this book, first of all I want to let you know that you are strong, stronger than you know right now. I have seen surviving spouses from diverse walks of life find the strength within themselves to carry on and handle the issues that must be addressed. You will get through it. It is difficult, but you will make it through. A great many other people have gone through this experience, and they have been okay.

I know your life doesn't seem normal right now; in fact, it's actually not normal. I hope that by helping you manage your new financial situation, this book will help restore some sense of normality to your life. I hope this book will give you the confidence to believe in time that you still can realize your dreams and financial goals, even though your spouse is no longer with you.

This book is intended as a useful guide, a reference source and workbook to help you make your way through the financial aspects of your new situation. I think of it as a little life preserver. If you are out there battered by a sea of grief and feeling overwhelmed by the financial decisions that you face, I'd like this book to help you stay afloat and heading toward shore.

Specifically, this book will help you identify the urgent financial matters that should be addressed right away. It will also help you sort out the other important tasks and decisions that can be set aside for now and tackled later—things that don't need to be done immediately, even if it feels like they do.

One theme I will stress is how important it is to have a good team in place to advise you. This book will provide suggestions for finding the members of your team and some tips on working with them. You can take this book with you when you meet with your advisors, and there are places for you to take notes when you're in those meetings.

Because it seems helpful to people going though this to be able to get something done and to see progress, this book also has a number of checklists for you to use. In addition to helping you get things organized, it may feel less overwhelming if you tackle issues one at a time, rather than grappling with everything at once.

I am also including several client stories. These case studies are composite views, compiled from my years of experience as a financial advisor. The names and some of the details of the clients' situations have been changed to protect their privacy. Their stories illustrate some strategies that were successful as well as some pitfalls to avoid.

These are examples only and are not intended to be recommendations. Every person's circumstances are unique, and your results may vary.

In addition to the case stories, in the course of writing this book I interviewed my mom and number of my clients and asked them what advice they would give to a good friend who had just lost a spouse. Thoughts they would like to share with you from their own experience are sprinkled throughout, in their own words.

# Chapter 1. The First Things You Should Do—Or Not Do

## Avoid making any long-term decisions

The loss of a spouse is a life-altering experience fraught with heart- wrenching emotional and financial adjustments. If you are in this position right now, the most important guideline to follow is: **Do not make any long-term legal or financial decisions**. In fact, don't make any major decisions within those first six months or so, except perhaps to interview professional advisors to find those you feel comfortable working with.

Your financial situation needs your full attention. When you are grieving or feeling the range of other emotions that accompany a great loss, it is very difficult to make sound financial decisions. There are some papers you may need to locate quickly, and you will need to meet with your advisors on some immediate issues. But it is better to delay any important long-term decisions until your thinking is less clouded by your emotions.

> ✎ *In her own words*
> *I'd have to say the first six months are strictly survival mode. Six months is an arbitrary number—for some people it takes longer than others. While you're in that shock phase, you can't think clearly enough to make any kind of decision. I remember not even being able to process really simple instructions. My advice would be to just hold off on everything. Don't be impulsive. Get through the shock phase before you try to do anything that's really important.*

In addition to delaying important decisions, there are several other helpful strategies to follow if you find yourself suddenly single:

## Take care of yourself and your loved ones

First, take care of yourself and your loved ones. It is only natural to experience emotional upheaval when going through this traumatic life passage. It is crucial that you give yourself time to grieve, feel your loss and adjust to your new circumstances. During this process, take steps to care for yourself and your loved ones.[1]

**Stay in charge of your own life**. Do not turn over decision-making responsibility to anyone, no matter how overwhelmed you feel and no matter how caring the person who volunteers to manage your affairs may seem to be.

**Drive with care**. When you are grieving, it's easy to become distracted. Use extra care when you are behind the wheel.

**Seek grief counseling for yourself and for your children** (if you are a parent). Your children are grieving too, and they need support. If you are resentful or angry, have separate grief sessions, without your children present.

**Maintain rituals**. Children experiencing the death of a parent are initially likely to feel abandoned and insecure. Maintaining established patterns of holidays, birthdays, Saturday outings, sporting events, and other family rituals will comfort them and provide them with a sense of normality and consistency.

**Follow a routine**. It may not be possible to have the same daily routine as before the death, but during this time, establishing a routine and sticking with it will help you and your family adjust.

**Nurture yourself**. Take care of your spiritual, emotional and physical needs. Nobody will do this for you. Eat healthy meals, exercise, take vitamins and continue any usual medications. Allow yourself to grieve, and don't rush the process. Give yourself as much time as you need to adjust to your new circumstances.

---

[1] A number of the following suggestions were adapted from an article on the mental- health-matters.com website written by Single Parent Central, www.singleparentcentral.com. Please see the Resources chapter at the end of this book for the complete reference.

---

✍ *In her own words*

*I could not go into my husband's closet and clean it out for over a year after he died, because I could smell the cologne he wore, and it was just too painful. I had people pressuring me, "You need to do this." But everybody is different. You can't have people pressuring you to do something you're not ready for. I know some people feel better "cleaning house," and that is their way of coping. But in my instance, I just couldn't do it. It took a year until I was ready, then I did it, and I was fine.*

---

## Expect emotional upheaval

In her classic book, *On Death and Dying*, Elisabeth Kubler-Ross identified five discrete stages of grief: denial, anger, bargaining, depression and acceptance. Knowing you are likely to experience these feelings during a time of loss, and realizing that they are normal, can be extremely helpful. The following descriptions were adapted from Kubler-Ross's book:[2]

**Denial**: *"I'm just fine." "This can't be real."* — People in this stage are full of disbelief and denial. You still expect your spouse to walk through the door.

**Anger**: *"It's not fair!" "Why me?" "Why did this happen?"* — Anger at the situation or at others is common. You may even feel anger at your deceased partner for dying.

**Bargaining**: *"I'll be a better person, if you'll bring him back."* — At this stage, you try to negotiate to change the situation. You might bargain with God to bring your spouse back.

**Depression**: *"Why bother?" "What's the use?"* — You realize the situation won't change. The death really happened, and there is no way to bring your partner back. Acknowledgement of the situation often brings depression.

**Acceptance**: *"I'll pull through." "I can't change it, so I may as well*

---

[2] These descriptions were adapted from an article on the mental-health-matters. com website which was written by Single Parent Central in which they adapted descriptions from Kubler-Ross's book. Please see the Resources chapter at the end of this book for the complete reference.

*get on with things.*" — While you haven't forgotten what occurred, at this stage you are ready to begin moving on with your life.

Kubler-Ross pointed out that not everyone goes through the stages in the same order, some people don't appear to go through all the stages and some people revisit stages when something triggers memories of the painful experience.

---

✑ *In her own words*

*Looking back, I wish it had been made more clear to me that it's normal not to be able to think straight. Then I would have known, "Okay. I'm okay." But I think for a while I thought I was losing my mind, because I was under so much stress.*

---

✑ *In her own words*

*Give yourself some slack if you forget things. Make yourself post-it notes or lists of things to do so that you won't forget. Don't try to rely on your memory because you won't have much of a memory. You may be very impulsive. You may get easily distracted and find it hard to stay focused. I think the best thing is to really slow down. There are some days when you just can't think. And that's okay.*

---

## Let yourself feel all of your feelings

Many times surviving spouses are fighting back tears when talking with me. Give yourself time to grieve. Let yourself go through this stage and to feel the full range of your emotions. As a surviving spouse in this situation, you just need to recognize that your highly emotional state will affect your ability to make sound decisions.

You may find yourself swamped by emotions while trying to solve complex financial problems. If you were not the one who handled the family's investments or made the long-term financial decisions, it can be a huge shock to realize that you must learn about a variety of financial subjects and make far-reaching decisions about your finances.

In addition, issues that most people take years to decide, you may be trying to resolve in a couple of days or months. This can seem overwhelming. You may also feel the pressure to make good decisions, because the actions you take now can determine the quality of the rest of your life.

You may need to decide:

- Do I sell or keep the house?
- Do I pay off the credit cards?
- How should I use the life insurance?
- Should I pay off the mortgage on the house?
- Will I have to go back to work?
- How will I pay for my children's college education?
- Should I relocate to be closer to family?

---

### ⌕ *In her own words*

*Just know that you've got a long road ahead of you. I don't want to make you feel awful, but there's a lot to learn. If you haven't done the paperwork before, it's overwhelming. I took notes on everything that I did. And I wanted to know what everything meant—property taxes, escrow, all of it. Maybe that's just the way I learn. I don't know. But I think it's important to understand what you're doing. So it's a long process. For me, it was.*

---

In some cases, a surviving spouse's situation is further complicated because the deceased hid things from her—like omitting to tell her they had huge credit card balances or forgetting to mention the fact that he took out a large loan against an insurance policy. So the widow might not have all the financial resources that she thought she had. If the deceased concealed aspects of their financial situation, the survivor can feel angry. It can also alter the high opinion she had of her spouse. And this can make her emotional state even more tumultuous.

In addition to grief and anger, you may experience fear and anxiety. Fear of the unknown. Fear of making the wrong decision. Fear of living a life without your spouse. Anxiety about who will take care of your children if something should happen to you. Fear of running out of money.

I find that people sometimes make decisions during this time of emotional turmoil that are either rash decisions or ones they look back on later and say, "Did I really decide to do that?"

Postpone every big decision you can, until you get through the initial shock, until you make some progress on working through your feelings and begin to heal, until you can think more clearly again.

---

✑ *In her own words*

*Acting too quickly is not advisable. Not only can you not think about what you're doing, you could make bad decisions. In my case, I probably would have lost $100,000 if I had traded in that stock when I thought I had to. I wanted to do things right away. That's not a good idea. But my gut feeling was, "I've just got to do this right now," because I had a high level of anxiety about getting things done.*

---

✑ *In her own words*

*Things will happen where you'll go, "Gosh, that's just not me— that's not normally something I would do." You're going to make a few boo- boos. It's just something that will happen. I got into an automobile accident. I pulled out of a parking lot and ran right into this man's car because my mind was not on driving. I was crying and ran right into him, and I felt so bad. I told the man, "My husband just passed away." At first he was ready to tear my head off because I had made a stupid move. But once I told him why I was having a really bad day, he was cooperative, and my insurance paid for the accident. I haven't had an accident since.*

---

## One big decision to postpone: your house

One of the most important decisions to postpone if you possibly can is "Where am I going to live?"

You may be deeply attached to your house, and your home can represent a security blanket. The questions of where you are going to live and whether you can afford to stay in your home can loom as over- riding concerns. Despite that, the issue of where you should live is not a decision you should try to reach right away.

If you can't imagine leaving your home, it may be a good indicator that you should stay there. On the other hand, if the house holds too many memories or painful feelings, it might be best to sell it and try to move on. But you won't know this overnight. You will only know after giving yourself time for your feelings to settle, after you have reached a point where you can calmly reflect and ponder your decision.

So I recommend that you put that decision off if you possibly can. If you can manage it financially, just continue to pay your bills and remain living where you are for the next three months to a year. A year would be ideal, but the longer you can stay there, the better.

That way at least you will know you have a place to live for the next period of time. If you know you can stay in your house for now, without having to decide about selling it or moving, it will free you from the anxiety around that huge decision and allow you to focus on other, more urgent things that should be addressed right away.

# *Rose's story*

Rose was a real estate agent who worked with her husband, Tom. When they were both in their early seventies, he passed away. Overwhelmed by grief, she couldn't focus.

In a vulnerable state and lacking financial savvy, Rose was talked into buying a number of long-term investment products by a broker at her bank. Unfortunately, at her stage in life, these long-term investments were not the best options for her. They were not going to give her the access and flexibility that she would need. Also, making these investments was not something that needed to be done right away. She made those decisions too soon. Later we had to withdraw from some of those products, and it ended up costing her some money.

Remember this: if the money is secure, even if it's sitting there in a bank account earning very little interest, you do not have to make a decision on it right away. Just let it sit there. The little bit of extra money you might get by finding a better interest rate or switching to a different financial product may cost you more money in the long run. Once emotions have subsided and the dust has settled, you may see that an investment that seemed attractive at the time was not the best one for you. It's very hard to make good long-term decisions while you are in emotional turmoil.

Rose eventually acknowledged her shortcomings when it came to financial matters and realized she needed to get professional advice independent of her bank, because the bank had a vested interest. At that point, she sought out someone she trusted, her nephew, who is very savvy financially. He happened to be a client of mine, so he came to me and said, "Hey, she needs our help. Let's go through it with her." Also, although he was the guiding force in getting her in to talk to me, he let her make her own decisions. That made him an excellent choice.

In our initial meetings, it became clear that Rose was worried that she needed to sell her condominium. Since she had enough liquid assets to meet her living expenses, I was able to talk her into staying in her condo for a while, to give her a chance to see if selling it was the right decision.

After we took the time to evaluate Rose's assets, we saw that it would be a good strategy to sell the house so that she could have a lifetime income stream. But we were able to postpone that decision for eight or nine months.

Once she came to grips with the fact that she needed to sell the house, she sold it, and the money came in. The decision to sell was made not in one appointment, not in two appointments, but in several appointments over the course of a year, and it was a good one. When Rose finally did sell the condo, she felt good about it.

Right now Rose is in a sound financial position. However, now that the housing market has dropped, she's been thinking about taking that money and buying another house while real estate prices are low. But I'm asking her, "At seventy-four years old, do you want a mortgage payment? Do you want to pay taxes and insurance? Do you want to take on the expense and responsibilities of homeownership? Or do you want to travel the world instead? Do you want to see your grandchildren? Do you want to retire in style and go out to dinner and treat people?" That is the choice she has to make. Having worked as a realtor, her ingrained belief is that real estate is the key to financial security. But at her age, she probably has a limited amount of time when she can really enjoy her life. Taking on a mortgage payment now will mean she won't be able to do many of the things she loves to do. So she's bouncing the idea off of different people now and thinking it over. It's not a decision she will be making overnight.

What Rose did well was she realized her lack of financial savvy. She searched out someone she trusted and knew had a good grasp of finances and included him in meetings with a financial professional. Then she came to her own decisions based on our meetings.

She made a mistake in rushing to make decisions on funds she didn't need to act on yet. She put herself in long-term investments that were not appropriate for her situation and incurred penalties to exit them. Rose is not the first widow to have made decisions within the first few months after her spouse died that she ended up having to undo later and pay the cost.

This illustrates one of the main themes of this book: wait. Let yourself breathe, let yourself cry, let yourself go through all the emotions of losing a loved one. You do not have to make long-term decisions a month after your spouse passes away. Just try to keep the day-to-day bills paid. Don't panic. And trust that it will work out.

## Your family, your friends and your finances

Many nice people will want to help you. Your family and friends will tell you what they think you should be doing and how they think you should be living. They mean well. They have the best intentions. But their lives are different than yours, their values are different than yours, and what they are feeling may not be what you are feeling. So when they suggest things to you, it will be from their own perspective.

---

### ☞ *In her own words*

*It can be a little delicate dealing with the helpers. I had people offering to help who really didn't know what they were doing. One friend of mine spent eight hours trying to help me figure out an insurance issue. Then my brother-in-law looked at it. It took him five minutes to figure out what I needed to do. I told him about my friend, almost in tears. He laughed, and then he almost started to cry, too.*

---

I strongly encourage you to think for yourself. I know it may be difficult right now when you are experiencing intense emotions. It's similar to getting heavy static on a phone line: you are trying to focus on one thing, but you have all this noise from your emotions, combined with all this noise from multiple people giving you their opinions. It can interfere with your mental functioning. At times you may find it hard to make even simple decisions. But even though your thinking and judgment are unavoidably skewed during this time, you will still have instincts about certain situations, and you should listen to them.

Sometimes you know deep down what your decision should be on a given issue, but it can be very difficult to express your preference and stick to it when other people are giving you advice. And believe me, when someone dies, friends and family come from all around to give you their opinions. Even if they didn't give you advice before, they will give it to you now.

I have seen that be a pitfall for many widows. They end up succumbing to pressure from others and doing what other people have told them to do, even when they aren't sure it is what *they* really want.

I don't mean professionals, but family and friends, who tend to be well meaning, but are not necessarily informed. Decisions made this way often end up being ones a widow regrets later on.

Also, you have lost your trusted partner, and it may be tempting to try to fill the gap with someone else—a family friend or professional advisor. Just be aware that you may be pulled in this direction, and be cautious.

Take your time when reaching decisions, and as much as you can, keep thinking for yourself.

---

*In her own words*

*You do get a lot of help from people. A lot of times, it's their way of dealing with the grief. I could tell that was going on with one neighbor friend. I was kind of trying to help him as he was trying to help me. He really stepped in, and that bothered some of the people around me. Some of my relatives said, "Your neighbor is kind of bossy," or, "Man, I don't agree with your neighbor." It didn't bother me though. That tells me that I really needed to depend on him, and he probably sensed that. It was only a bit later when people were just walking into my house without even knocking that I thought, "Okay. I'm ready to set some boundaries." I even told one neighbor, "You know, I might be walking around nude in my house. So just make sure you knock before you come in."*

---

*In her own words*

*You have to make sure that you are the one in charge and that you are understanding what's going on with your life and your finances. I had a husband who was controlling. When you entrust your family member or friend to help you handle things, you have to be very careful that they don't take over where your spouse might have left off. It's advantageous that someone steps in and helps, but when they continue to control things and don't allow you to start to take charge, that can be detrimental. You can let someone take hold at the beginning but you can't let them continue indefinitely. You need to be able to take control yourself.*

---

### ❧ For Family & Friends: How to Be Useful to a Surviving Spouse

Whether you are a family member, friend or neighbor, of course you want to help, and the new widow needs your support. Here are a few things to keep in mind and some ways you can be most useful:

- Realize that she is in a highly emotional state and that this might affect her thinking. Be patient. You may need to explain things more than once.
- As much as possible, support her inthinking things through for herself and making her own decisions. Provide information, and listen well. But do not make the final decisions for her.
- Be available to go along on interviews with advisor candidates and on meetings with the advisors she chooses. Take notes so that you can be her "back-up memory" if she wants to review things later.
- Support her in postponing major decisions until she is through the first stages of grieving and can begin to take charge of her life again.
- Run interference to screen out those who might seek to take advantage of her more vulnerable state for their own gain.
- Encourage her to think about her future needs and goals as soon as she is able to do so.

## Chapter 1 Recap

- Avoid making any long-term legal or financial decisions.
- Take care of yourself and your loved ones.
- Expect to be in a state of emotional upheaval.
- Give yourself time to grieve and feel all of your feelings.
- Accept that your emotional state will affect your ability to think clearly, and be kind and patient with yourself.
- Postpone any decision about moving or selling your house as long as you can.
- Accept the help of your family and friends, but continue to think for yourself, take charge of your life, and make your own decisions as much as possible

## Sylvia's Story

A year after her first marriage ended in divorce, Sylvia went to her class reunion and found Arthur, her high-school sweetheart, there. One thing led to another: she moved from Virginia to California to be with him, and they got married soon after.

Arthur was a highly successful entrepreneur and businessman. He and Sylvia came to me for financial planning shortly after they married, and we were in the process of working on a plan for them as a couple when Arthur died suddenly in a car accident.

Sylvia was devastated. She had been swept off her feet and was deeply in love, then was dealt this crushing blow. I remember her sitting in my office unable to stop crying. That was seven or eight years ago, and she is still grieving.

Compounding her emotional trauma, Sylvia had no understanding of their financial situation and little previous experience handling finances. Knowing this, she sought professional financial help, a good decision on her part.

However, there were other people involved she believed she could trust because they had been friends of her husband's and were people he trusted. Unfortunately, one of those people took advantage of her, which was not difficult for him to do because of her lack of financial sophistication. He appropriated funds that should have gone to Sylvia, and he was never indicted for this misappropriation. Sylvia just lost that money. In retrospect, she realized it was a serious mistake to have placed so much trust in that person.

Another person befriended her in an overpowering way. This woman inserted herself aggressively into Sylvia's finances and involved herself in Sylvia's decision-making. In one instance, Sylvia had a very concentrated position in one stock. I suggested she sell that stock and diversify, which I felt was the proper diagnosis for her situation. She agreed it made sense. Then Sylvia called me at home over the weekend to tell me she no longer wanted to sell the stock. It seemed odd for her to be saying that, because she knew hardly anything about stocks. What had happened? Well, her new friend had convinced her not to sell—even though that person had no financial background.

Because Sylvia was struggling emotionally, other people in her life tried to take over and were very insistent that Sylvia follow their advice. She was easily swayed; she had always been a person of modest means, and now all of a sudden she was worth millions of dollars because of Arthur.

I usually encourage surviving spouses to take someone with them to meetings with their advisors. It's good to have another person listening and have someone to review things with later. The danger is this outside party then becomes privy to all the details of the survivor's financial situation. Sometimes these outside parties have personal motives and hidden agendas and put their own interests above those of the surviving spouse.

Sylvia never did listen to my advice to sell that concentrated stock position and diversify. And unfortunately, the stock went to zero during the tech downturn. The only thing she had left was her house, which we had completely paid off from the life insurance.

The only reason Sylvia was living in California now was Arthur—she had no family here. So over the course of a year, we talked a lot about whether she wanted to move back home to Virginia, to be closer to her family. During this time, she was having family members come out to California to visit her. Guess who was paying for that? Sylvia was. She was paying her family's phone bills. She was paying their credit card bills. She was even paying people's gambling debts. Everyone who knew she had inherited money got in line for a handout. And it was very difficult for her to say no.

Widows are especially vulnerable. Here is the reply I think surviving spouses should have on hand to use when people appear and ask for loans or gifts: "The money is tied up. I can't really get to it." That's a very useful response, and people understand it.

Sylvia eventually sold her house and moved back to Virginia. Since the stock was gone, the proceeds from selling the house represented the bulk of the money that remains for her to live on for the rest of her life. I recommended she buy the house in Virginia outright, and she did. But her friends and family convinced her to do extensive remodeling—changes that the house didn't really need—and that added another $50,000 to her housing cost.

In the last several years, Sylvia's money has diminished much faster than we had planned—primarily because of her inability to say no. Family means so much to her that whatever her family members ask for, she almost always gives. But recently I had to tell her, "Sylvia, you have got to stop this steady withdrawal or your money is not going to last long enough." So she has now stopped taking money out and has started to focus on living a simpler life. And she realizes she must learn how to say no.

Sylvia is also someone who finds it hard to save. If there is money in her account, she will spend it. If you know that about yourself, consult with a financial advisor and share your situation, so he or she can help protect you from yourself. There are financial products that will give you a flat monthly stipend, instead of giving you access to a huge amount of money when people come asking you for things.

# Chapter 2: Immediate Issues That Should Be Addressed

So far my advice has been to postpone all the major decisions you can until the first shock has passed, until you are starting to recover your equilibrium and you can think more clearly. However, there are some matters that need to be taken care of immediately. What are those urgent issues, the ones that can't wait?

## The urgent issues

- Collecting all your paperwork and getting an accurate picture of your complete financial situation
- Surrounding yourself with a team of trusted professionals: a financial advisor, an attorney, and a CPA or other tax professional
- Obtaining death certificates
- Notifying life insurance and other insurance companies
- Ensuring that your health insurance continues and applying for COBRA if needed
- Paying any taxes that are coming due, such as property taxes and income taxes, for example

## Create an accurate snapshot of your complete financial situation

You must have an accurate picture of where you stand right now financially in order to make sound decisions going forward. Organize your paperwork as soon as you can. As you go through your spouse's papers, **don't throw away anything even remotely connected to your finances**. Collect the 401K statements, the IRA statements, the life insurance statements, the credit card bills, the property tax bills, the income tax returns—everything you can find that has to do with your finances.

Keep everything you've found in one large box or folder, for example a plastic file box with a handle, available at any office supply store. You will need this information when you meet with your advisors. Having all the paperwork together will make it easier for you and your advisors to locate and refer to the necessary documents and to contact other parties through the information on their statements. See page 23 for a list of important papers to locate and have on hand for your advisors.

---

*⬧ In her own words*

*Another important area is going through all your paperwork, as painful as it can be. And don't throw anything away. You never know. I've had people come into the bank where I work, and they'll say, "Well, I went in and I started cleaning and I threw out something I really needed for my taxes." Sometimes people find an insurance policy that their spouse tucked in a drawer and forgot they had. Go through your safe deposit box. Go through all of your papers. And keep everything.*

---

**A contemporary caution**: With so much banking and bill paying conducted online these days, surviving spouses may face a new challenge. If the deceased person didn't share the passwords for online accounts, it can be much harder to locate the information you need. You may need to consult your financial advisor and attorney for help in this situation.

## CHECKLIST

**Important papers to have on hand before meeting with your advisors:**

- ☐ Copies of joint tax returns for the past five years
- ☐ Copies of your and your spouse's retirement accounts, i.e. 401k, 403b and TSA
- ☐ All insurance policies, including home, auto, life, health, long-term care, and disability
- ☐ Current statements for all brokerage accounts, including IRAs and Roth IRAs
- ☐ Current statements of mutual fund holdings
- ☐ The deed to your home
- ☐ Your most recent mortgage statement
- ☐ Any trust documents
- ☐ Any business partnership agreements
- ☐ Birth certificates
- ☐ Death certificates, ten to twenty certified copies
- ☐ Marriage certificate
- ☐ List of credit cards
- ☐ Titles or lease agreements to autos, motor homes and boats
- ☐ Employer stock options
- ☐ Wills
- ☐ Living wills and trust documents
- ☐ Military discharge papers
- ☐ List of assets

## Assemble your team of trusted advisors

One of the first few things I recommend you do is to surround yourself with a team of professionals you can trust. By handling matters on your own or relying solely on friends and family for help, you increase the odds that you will make mistakes that professionals would catch.

Also, professional advisors will not be in an emotional state. They will be able to examine your situation objectively. They can point out areas you may not even be aware of and help you make decisions about those matters. They can advocate for your best interests in the face of conflicting advice from other people.

In addition, getting a team in place will allow you to discuss ideas with someone else. Most couples bounce ideas back and forth before making a big decision, and you have lost your partner in that process. Using experienced professionals as a sounding board will allow you to make better decisions.

Through all of this, your goal should not be to have your team make the decisions for you, but to have them inform you and support you in reaching your own decisions. They will provide information, insights and recommendations based on their experience and expertise. But as much as possible, you still need to make the decisions yourself.

I recommend that your team include a CPA or tax professional, a financial advisor and an attorney.

When assembling your team, get referrals from people you trust. Think of the people you know who have a lot of money or are astute financial managers. Ask them who they would use in your situation. In the next chapter, I'll go into more detail on how to choose the right advisors.

---

*In her own words*

*What happens when you're trying to make wise decisions is that you don't have anyone to work things through with anymore. So if you could find a good friend or a good financial advisor, somebody you trust and who's versed in this type of thing, that will help.*

---

## ADVISOR RECOMMENDATIONS

Notes on professionals recommended to you by family, friends or associates to be your attorney, CPA, and/or financial advisor:

Recommended by: _____

Type of professional advisor: _____

Name: _____

Contact information

Address: _____

_____

Phone: _____

Email address: _____

Why they were recommended: _____

_____

_____

_____

Recommended by: _____

Type of professional advisor: _____

Name: _____

Contact information

Address: _____

_____

Phone: _____

Email address: _____

Why they were recommended: _____

_____

_____

_____

## ADVISOR RECOMMENDATIONS

Notes on professionals recommended to you by family, friends or associates to be your attorney, CPA, and/or financial advisor:

Recommended by: _____

Type of professional advisor: _____

Name: _____

Contact information

Address: _____

_____

Phone: _____

Email address: _____

Why they were recommended: _____

_____

_____

_____

Recommended by: _____

Type of professional advisor: _____

Name: _____

Contact information

Address: _____

_____

Phone: _____

Email address: _____

Why they were recommended: _____

_____

_____

_____

## ADVISOR RECOMMENDATIONS

Notes on professionals recommended to you by family, friends or associates to be your attorney, CPA, and/or financial advisor:

Recommended by: _____

Type of professional advisor: _____

Name: _____

Contact information

Address: _____

_____

Phone: _____

Email address: _____

Why they were recommended: _____

_____

_____

_____

Recommended by: _____

Type of professional advisor: _____

Name: _____

Contact information

Address: _____

_____

Phone: _____

Email address: _____

Why they were recommended: _____

_____

_____

_____

## Death certificates

One task you should take care of right away is sending off for copies of the death certificate. And order more than you think you will need (I recommend getting 10 to 20) because each time you request something from an entity like a bank or an insurance company, they're going to say, "We need a death certificate." That can delay everything, so it's important to have enough copies on hand.

In most states, copies are available for a fee through the local coroner's office. The funeral parlor should be able to handle this for you on a straight pass-through basis. As of this writing in 2009, the fee was $12 for each certified copy in Santa Clara County, California.

## Life insurance

To get life insurance policies paid, you will need to notify the insurance company that the covered person has passed away, and you will need to send them the death certificate. Depending on the insurance company, the process of applying for and receiving payment on a policy can take anywhere from a week to six weeks. So the sooner you can get those out, the better.

---

*⌦ In her own words*

*I would strongly encourage you not to spend money that you haven't actually received yet, because sometimes you might be expecting a certain amount, but that may not end up being what you get. For instance, we had an insurance policy for $5000 that I bought for my husband at my job. Because it was a term life policy and had been recently purchased, it did not have $5,000 in value yet. Now I could have gone out buying things thinking, "I'm going to be getting that $5,000 check"—and then lo and behold, I get a check for $2,500 and I'm behind the eight ball. That can cause more stress. So, don't count on getting any money until it comes. It's amazing how many times there will be commissions taken out or other fees, and you could end up getting a lot less than you were expecting.*

---

## COBRA transitional health insurance

Federal laws in the United States provide for the spouse and family of a deceased person to continue existing health coverage for thirty-six months through COBRA. This transitional insurance is very important, because you never want to be without health insurance. You should apply for COBRA coverage, if you need it, as soon as possible after the death of your spouse. Since your spouse's employer is no longer subsidizing the cost of health insurance, you will have to pay the full premium yourself. But you will be able to keep your existing health insurance intact during this transitional period.

After COBRA expires, you will need to secure your own health insurance coverage. Because you must have a clear head to consider the wide variety of health insurance options that are available and their costs, you don't want to try to do that while your mind is muddled. One of the benefits of COBRA is that it gives you breathing room— time to research the health insurance options open to you and your family, time to apply to the provider you choose, and time to put your ongoing health care coverage in place.

## Taxes

If tax payments are due soon, meeting deadlines is critical in order to avoid interest charges and penalties. Depending on the time of year, you may need to file an extension on income taxes. There may be property taxes to pay. If your spouse was self-employed, estimated tax payments may be owed. Your CPA or tax professional can help you distinguish the urgent matters from those that can wait a while.

Even if you've done your own taxes in the past, it's important to consult a professional now, because there are financial issues associated with a death that are more complex than doing a standard tax return. Your tax situation may have changed. The death of a spouse can impact a number of areas that may have tax ramifications, such as the transfer of titles to property, business ownership, future property tax liabilities, minimum IRA distributions and survivor Social Security benefits, to name a few.

Consulting with a tax professional now can save you money in the long run. Especially in the first year after your spouse's death, your CPA or tax accountant will be able to provide substantial assistance, helping you to weigh your options and make the wisest decisions.

## Stock options and positions

If you have stock options, you may need to decide whether to execute them, and there may be deadlines involved. If your portfolio includes substantial positions in volatile companies and/or highly concentrated positions in one company, you may want to diversify sooner rather than later. Your financial advisor will be able to help you weigh your options.

## Chapter 2 Recap

- Create an accurate snapshot of your complete financial situation.
- Collect your important papers as soon as you can (see page 23). Having a dedicated box for those is helpful.
- As you go through paperwork, don't throw away anything even remotely connected to your finances.
- If you don't already have a trusted financial advisor, attorney and CPA or other tax professional, get recommendations from the people you know who are the most financially savvy.
- Obtain an adequate number of death certificates.
- Notify life insurance companies and start the process of getting payment on any policies.
- Ensure continuing health care insurance coverage for you and your minor children, and apply for COBRA if needed.
- Pay all taxes that are coming due, to avoid incurring interest charges and penalties.
- Decide whether to execute stock options and/or to diversify concentrated stock positions.

## Cheryl's Story

Cheryl and John were married for nearly forty years and were clients of mine for the last eight or nine of those. In the last five years of his life John suffered from Lou Gehrig's disease (ALS), which we all knew would end in his death. Their marriage had been based on traditional roles, and Cheryl gave up her personal life to devote herself to John's care during his illness.

After John was diagnosed, because we knew that John's condition was terminal, each time I met with them I tried to share with Cheryl that, "What we are doing now is based on the two of you being married, and this is the amount of income that you need now. But if and when John passes away, I think we need to change the portfolio." It turned out this was not something Cheryl could think about beforehand.

Then after John died, I wanted her to come in about a month after the funeral. It was too soon. She didn't make her appointment. She didn't want to come in. She didn't want to talk about the money issues. I learned something from that. Even though we knew in advance that John was going to die, Cheryl still needed to go through the grieving process when he eventually did pass away. It was six or seven months before we actually got together. And it ended up being almost a year to the day after he passed away that we actually changed her investment portfolio to reflect her needs in her new situation. Looking back on John's prolonged illness, even though Cheryl knew what his fate would be, when he eventually died her mourning process was no different from those whose spouses died unexpectedly.

In addition to their home, Cheryl and John also owned a rental house. After John died, Cheryl sold their home, the house she had lived in for almost forty years, and moved into the rental property. This decision was based solely on the tax implications. From a tax point of view, it made sense for her to sell the house because she didn't have to pay capital gains on the sale. It would benefit her tax situation and also benefit her heirs.

However, even though she knew logically that selling the house was a good thing to do, she was still emotionally attached to her home, and she regretted the decision later. The lesson here is that sometimes, even though it makes sense on paper, a decision may not be the best one for you personally. In my experience, trying to make decisions based on taxes alone is sometimes not the best way to proceed. You need to be at peace with the decision in your heart as well as in your head.

Fortunately, when Cheryl sold the house, she carried the loan to derive some income from the estate. The buyers eventually defaulted on the loan, and she had to foreclose on the property. Cheryl moved back in, and the last time I spoke with her she sounded much more content now that she is back in the home she loves.

One thing Cheryl has done right is that she's always brought one or both of her sons with her to our meetings. They come to the appointments, and they listen. I think she's fortunate to have included them, especially because they don't tell her what she should do, but instead try to support her decision- making process.

The last thing I'll mention about Cheryl is that because she had cared for her husband for so long, she knew deep in her heart that she needed to do things for herself once he passed away. She got more active in her gardening club and volunteered at a local hospital. She took time for herself, and that was another thing she did well while going through this process.

***In her own words***

*I want to encourage you that it's not always going to be this painful, that you will learn to deal with it. You may not ever get over the loss completely, but you'll learn to live with it.*

# Chapter 3: Your Advisor Team

## Finding your advisors

You may be fortunate enough to have a trusted financial advisor, attorney and tax professional already in your corner. If you do, you will want tomakesure thatthese individuals have experience helping people in your situation. If you don't have these professional relationships in place, then you will want to surround yourself with a team of qualified professionals you can trust.

To find good candidates, ask the people you know who are the most financially astute who they would go to if they were in your shoes. You are looking for advisors who have had experience with other people in your situation, individuals who have helped many other people deal with their financial affairs after the death of a spouse.

It's also important to find people who are good listeners, who can grasp your situation and reiterate what you are saying. At times the most useful "advice" will be good listening that allows you to think things through for yourself.

You will want to interview and carefully evaluate the professionals you are considering as part of your team. Interview several candidates if you can, in person. Many professionals will not charge for an initial interview. Take a friend or family member with you to the interviews. Ask yourself if you learned something from talking with this person and if he or she seemed like someone who would take the time to educate you. Then choose the candidate who seems the most qualified and with whom you feel most comfortable.

If an advisor is reluctant to have you bring someone with you, take that as a clear signal that this is not the right person for you.

Your advisors should want to meet with the other professionals on your team. They should want to collaborate. They should want to talk to your family and hear all the different opinions. That way they can gain a more complete picture of your situation and will be able to advise you from a fully informed perspective.

Try to avoid people who have a vested interest in selling you something, for example an investment product, because that will affect their ability to give you objective advice.

You shouldn't necessarily trust the first person you meet either. Unfortunately, when some people see a widow, especially if there are substantial financial resources involved, they tend to think more about how they can profit rather than about what the widow needs. If you find someone who seems too eager, if a red flag goes up for you, trust your instincts and avoid that person.

### Choosing a financial advisor

Before you engage a financial professional, you should know what services the professional can provide, how much those services will cost and how the professional will get paid. A financial professional who is strictly an investment advisor may be limited to a narrow range of services and financial products that he or she is able to offer. And not all financial professionals are required to adhere to the same fiduciary standards that require that they put the client's interests ahead of their own. I recommend you look for a financial planner who is qualified to evaluate every aspect of your financial life and who can help you develop a comprehensive financial plan.

Here are some questions you should ask the candidates you are considering as your financial advisor:

- What experience do you have with people in my situation?
- What are your professional qualifications? What certifications and licenses do you hold? Are you registered with any regulatory agencies, such asthe SEC or FINRA (Financial Industry Regulatory Authority)?
- What products and services can you provide?

- Are you limited in the number and types of products or services you can offer? And if so, why?
- What is your approach to financial planning?
- How do you get paid for your services—hourly rate, flat fee or commission? What is your typical charge for one in my situation?
- Will I be working with others in your office or only with you? Can I meet the other people I may be working with?
- Haveyouever been disciplined byaregulatory agency for unethical or improper conduct or been sued by an unhappy client?

In addition to professional qualifications and experience, I believe the best financial advisor is someone who has the heart of a teacher. I say that because you will be sharing information that you used to share with your husband. You will be entering into an intimate long-term relationship where trust is required. And you will need his or her patience, understanding and ability to communicate clearly while you are in an emotional state. Look for someone who seems truly willing to help you through the process of sorting out your finances and can educate you along the way.

## A word on how financial advisors get paid

Before you decide on your financial advisor, make sure you understand how that person will get paid. Financial advisors can be compensated in several ways:

- A commission on the securities sold
- A percentage of the value of the assets managed
- An hourly fee for the time spent working for you
- A fixed fee for specified services
- Some combination of the above

Each compensation method has its potential benefits and possible conflicts of interest.

**Commission-based compensation.**Being paid on commission is the traditional model: you buy a stock; you pay the advisor a commission. Commission-based compensation creates the potential for a conflict of interest, as your advisor may be compensated only when changes are made to your portfolio. Some believe this encourages unnecessary transactions which incur commission charges. If your advisor works on a commission basis only, be sure their recommendations are based on your needs, not theirs.

**Assets-based fee compensation.** Many people, depending on their assets, choose an advisor who is working for an assets-based fee. The fee is based on how much money you have. If you have a million dollars in assets, the advisor will charge you a percent of that total to manage those assets on a yearly basis. The percentages vary.

One word of caution: there are many ways that fees can be "hidden," and this can make it hard to compare the fees you may be quoted from different advisors. Advisor A might tell you, "I charge 1 percent." But there could be hidden fees that weren't disclosed, bringing your total fees up to around 3 percent. Advisor B might say, "I charge 1.9 percent," and you might think advisor A would be the better choice. But in reality, if there are no hidden fees with Advisor B, the 1.9 percent fee would be much better than the actual 3 percent you would end up paying to Advisor A. You want to make sure that you are comparing apples to apples. So ask about hidden fees.

**Fee-based compensation.** The third option is the fee-only planner. This type of financial advisor has studied and received certification as a Certified Financial Planner.™ In this case, you pay the advisor a flat fee to prepare a financial plan for you. The fee varies depending on the complexity of your situation.

Afteryou meetwithe financial planner, he creates anindividualized plan. In most cases, financial planners are not asset managers—they will not put the investment strategies in place. Once the plan is completed, it is up to you either to find an advisor who will charge you to implement the strategies or to implement them yourself.

## Your involvement

One question you need to think through carefully before entering into an advisory relationship is how involved you want to be in managing your assets. If you are familiar with managing finances and investing and are in a frame of mind where you can focus on it right now, you can go to a fee-based financial planner, get a plan, and implement it yourself. On the other hand, if you lack the background and experience to implement a financial plan yourself, making and managing investments, or if you are not in a state of mind right now where you want to take that on, then you will be better off with someone who can implement the plan for you.

## My recommendation

Based on my experience with the widows I have worked with, I recommend that you choose an asset-based fee advisor who is also a Certified Financial Planner. A professional who has both of these qualifications can create a financial plan for you based on your needs and resources and can then implement and manage the plan for you, keeping your overall picture and goals in mind.

## Further information

The Resources section at the end of this book lists some good sources of comprehensive information on choosing a financial planner, how financial advisors get paid, the inherent conflicts of interest, and how to check a professional's disciplinary history.

## A final word of warning

Those who have just lost a spouse, especially if it was unexpected, generally are in a vulnerable state. It's a sad fact that there will be some people who will try to take advantage of that vulnerability, both in professional and personal relationships. Some people may look at your estate and see only dollar signs and how they might benefit.

So even though your emotions may be clouding your thinking, you need to have your radar up and be on your guard. To some interviews and initial meetings, you may not want to bring all the documents that reveal how much you are worth. Avoiding financial predators is another good reason you should take someone you trust with you to meetings.

---

*⬧ **In her own words***

*It's wonderful if you can have a financial advisor or someone you respect and trust, because to be very honest, if you have money, people can take advantage of you, and they can sell you something or get you to do something that will pad their pocket and not be in your best interest.*

---

## *Emma's Story*

Emma and Todd fell in love in college and were married for twenty years. Both of them were athletic and in great shape. One fall day, Todd went for a mountain bike ride with a group of friends. The fork on his bicycle snapped as he negotiated a rocky patch, and he was thrown over the handlebars, landed wrong and cracked his head. He died on the way to the hospital. At that instant, Emma's life was turned inside out.

Todd was the one who had handled their finances, and he'd done a good job. He had life insurance. He had college savings plans for their three children. He had stock options. He had several different savings accounts. The problem was that things were scattered all over the place.

I suggested to Emma that she first just get everything together and also that we meet every week and try to get something done financially each time. So we did that, and we started with the things that were most important. One of those was the life insurance.

Todd had several life insurance policies. We got all them all together, sent them out to the insurance companies, and she started receiving checks. The question then arose, "What should we do with these checks?" The highest priority in Emma's mind was to pay off the house.

She had about $250,000 left on the mortgage. But she and Todd had just started some remodeling projects, and there was work on the kitchen and landscaping that still needed to be finished. This was something she and Todd and been doing together, and she really wanted to see it through. But she also had a strong desire to pay off the house. And she wanted to travel with her children. We needed to see if she would be able to do all those things financially.

On the issue of paying off the house, I kept trying to tell Emma, "This may not be the time to make that decision. Why don't we get the remodeling finished the way you like it first. And then we'll see if you want to pay it off." But over the course of a year, I got the impression that paying off the house would give her the security blanket she needed to be able to carry on, care for her children and accomplish her goals. Before Todd died, paying off the house wasn't important to her. But after he passed away, the thought was constantly running through her mind, "I think my life would be better if I paid the house off."

So, a year later, we did pay off the house. Waiting that year gave her enough time to thoroughly consider whether she wanted to continue to live there or move someplace else. And I think when we paid off the house her life really changed.

In many cases, paying off the house is not the best financial decision, and many financial planners would discourage it. But in Emma's case it allowed her to focus on everything else. It was a freeing moment for her to walk into the bank and write a check and not owe them anything anymore. The clients I work with who have their houses paid off are able to live differently. For instance, if you don't have a mortgage payment, you have more options if you go back to work. You can get the job you would most enjoy doing, without having to worry so much about how much it pays.

After the house, Emma's next big decision was funding college for the kids. Looking back, Emma realized that she and Todd probably hadn't started early enough in planning for their children's education. Once we saw that the accounts they had been putting money into did not have sufficient funds to meet her children's college needs, we had to look at the other assets to see if the value of the life insurance, stocks and investment accounts could accommodate both ensuring Emma's security over the rest of her lifetime and funding college. We also needed to see if Emma could remain in a situation where she didn't have to go back to work, at least not initially.

As we looked at the stock portfolio, one issue emerged that I considered urgent: Emma had a substantial amount of stock in a very volatile company. We had to decide whether to sell all that stock and diversify, sell part of it, or keep all of it and assume the risk of a highly concentrated stock position. The fact that this stock represented the lion's share of her overall portfolio and the fact that it was in a volatile company made this a decision that couldn't be put off for long. If something happened to lower the stock's value, it could adversely affect Emma's future income. In the end, we did sell the stock and diversify her portfolio. The investments we made produced enough income to fund her children's college educations.

In this decision and others, Emma had many people helping her. In many ways she loved it, and it was great. But she also struggled with it. Because there were always friends and family there trying to help and advising her, it made it harder for her to think about what she really wanted and come to her own decisions. That was one reason why she needed to take her time on making the bigger decisions that were not urgent, such as paying off the house.

It's been three or four years now. Emma has taken her children to Europe and on a train trip across the country, trips that brought them all closer. Her oldest child is now going to college with the money we put aside for that. She has paid off her house. She is in a position where she still does not need to work, though she knows that she might want to one day. She is in a solid financial position going forward, because she has no credit card debt. In fact, she has no debt at all.

She still grieves from time to time, but no longer every day. I think if Emma were sitting here talking with us, she would say that the process of getting something done every week was therapeutic. It helped her to have that checklist and to be able to cross things off. She took her time making some of those big decisions. And she's in a strong position now financially.

It turns out the stock in that volatile company went up, not down, and she's not as wealthy as she would have been if she had held on to it. But she doesn't like to think about it that way. We accomplished her most important goals by diversifying her stock portfolio. And it took away the stress of worrying about what the stock would do. It allowed her to focus on her children, traveling with them and getting them to college. It's hard to put a dollar figure on her financial confidence.

**Working with your advisor team**

After you've chosen an advisor and are ready to go to work with them, once again take someone you trust with you to the meetings. The professional you meet with—your attorney or CPA or financial advisor—will cover an hour's worth of information, and you may retain ten minutes of it. Because you are in an intense emotional state, you can't expect your brain to be functioning normally. A friend or family member can be quite helpful as a back-up memory, someone you can check back with later to ask, "I think this is what he said. Is that what you heard?"

> ◌ *In her own words*
>
> *One of the areas I really had a problem was reading contracts and other papers. Take along a family member or a friend, and have them read it to you. You can say to them, "You know, I read this thing over, and this is what I think it says. But can you look at it? Maybe you will see something that I'm missing."*

**Checklists and Time Lines**

I have learned that when so many emotions are swirling around, if we can create action, most of the time it will alleviate much of the anxiety and fear. I find it helpful to meet with a surviving spouse weekly and see if we can accomplish one thing each week. It could be organizing the papers and getting everything together in one place. It could be ordering the death certificates. It could be tackling unpaid bills. Large or small, each step is a victory.

Having a checklist for daily/weekly tasks helps. Having time lines for the longer run, targeting what you can try to get done by certain months, also helps. Your advisors can assist you to set target dates and create a time line. They might say, "Let's see if we can make this decision in three months and this one in six months, or nine months, or a year from now." That way you can focus on one thing at a time, instead of being overwhelmed by the whole picture.

There will be times when you look at your checklist and think,

"I just can't do it this week." Sometimes when you are going through things, maybe credit card statements with items from the vacation you went on earlier in the year, memories and emotions will well up and you will have to stop. That's okay. Most of the time the checklist and time line will help you focus and feel less stressed. Of course, they need to be flexible. You will want to revise them as you go along and as you reach clarity on different issues.

---

✎ *In her own words*

*I'm a very regimented person, so I deal well with structure, like having a set time every week to meet with Brad. Any time something stressed me out, I put it in Brad's box. I had a place where I could put all the issues I had to go over with Brad or ask him about. I took the box to our meetings, so I knew we would get to it when I talked with him. I could put it aside and forget about it, because it's in Brad's box. And even if we didn't deal with it at one meeting, it stayed in the box until we dealt with it.*

*In fact, I would recommend that you have a box where you put anything that feels difficult—because every little thing can stress you out. It can be life insurance. It can be health insurance. Something that, in normal times, you'd say, "I'll just deal with it later," can be a real source of anxiety. So I'd recommend having a box with a label on it, like "Brad's Box." I had one for my attorney, too, "Larry's Box." I put the things for him in there, and I knew I would get to them when I saw him.*

*The box became a physical manifestation of some of my anxieties. It let me put them out of my mind. I think that would be the best advice I could give you. Just put it in the box.*

---

## DAILY/WEEKLY TASKS

Week of: _____

Goals for this week: _____

_____

_____

_____

_____

Monday: _____

_____

Tuesday: _____

_____

Wednesday: _____

_____

Thursday: _____

_____

Friday: _____

_____

Saturday: _____

_____

Sunday: _____

_____

# DAILY/WEEKLY TASKS

Week of: _____

Goals for this week: _____

_____

_____

_____

_____

Monday: _____

_____

Tuesday: _____

_____

Wednesday: _____

_____

Thursday: _____

_____

Friday: _____

_____

Saturday: _____

_____

Sunday: _____

_____

## DAILY/WEEKLY TASKS

Week of: _____

Goals for this week: _____

_____

_____

_____

_____

Monday: _____

_____

Tuesday: _____

_____

Wednesday: _____

_____

Thursday: _____

_____

Friday: _____

_____

Saturday: _____

_____

Sunday: _____

_____

## DAILY/WEEKLY TASKS

Week of: _____

Goals for this week: _____

_____

_____

_____

_____

Monday: _____

_____

Tuesday: _____

_____

Wednesday: _____

_____

Thursday: _____

_____

Friday: _____

_____

Saturday: _____

_____

Sunday: _____

_____

## DAILY/WEEKLY TASKS

Week of: _____

Goals for this week: _____

_____

_____

_____

_____

Monday: _____

_____

Tuesday: _____

_____

Wednesday: _____

_____

Thursday: _____

_____

Friday: _____

_____

Saturday: _____

_____

Sunday: _____

_____

## TIME LINE

What I want to complete in three months, six months, nine months, a year:

To have done in three months: _____

_____

_____

_____

_____

_____

_____

_____

_____

_____

_____

_____

To have done in six months: _____

_____

_____

_____

_____

_____

_____

_____

_____

_____

_____

_____

## TIME LINE

What I want to complete in three months, six months, nine months, a year:

To have done in three months: _____

_____

_____

_____

_____

_____

_____

_____

_____

_____

_____

_____

To have done in six months: _____

_____

_____

_____

_____

_____

_____

_____

_____

_____

_____

_____

## QUESTIONS TO ASK YOUR FINANCIAL ADVISOR

- Do I have enough income to last me so that I don't have to go back to work, or must I continue to work?
- Can I take six months off? Or a year off? What are my options?
- Can I afford to stay in my house long-term?
- Are my investments adequate to meet my new financial needs and goals?
- How much should I contribute to my children's education funds?
- How can I fund my retirement?
- Is my insurance coverage adequate to meet my current needs?
- Will my children receive adequate benefits should something happen to me?
- What can I get done in the next week?
- What do I need to get done in the next month, the next year?

NOTES: _____

_____

_____

_____

_____

_____

_____

_____

_____

_____

_____

_____

_____

_____

## QUESTIONS TO ASK YOUR ACCOUNTANT

- What licenses or designations do you have?
- How long have you been in the tax business?
- What tax issues do you specialize in?
- Do you have the knowledge and experience to handle my tax situation?
- What are your fees?
- Do you perform the work personally? If you outsource your work, what is the review process? Who signs the returns?
- Approximately how long will it take to finish my taxes?
- What is your privacy policy? Will you share my tax information with any third parties?
- Do you believe I'm paying too much, too little, or just the right amount of tax?

NOTES: _____

_____

_____

_____

_____

_____

_____

_____

_____

_____

_____

_____

_____

_____

_____
_____
_____
_____
_____
_____
_____
_____
_____
_____
_____
_____
_____
_____
_____
_____
_____
_____
_____
_____
_____
_____
_____
_____
_____
_____
_____

# QUESTIONS TO ASK YOUR ATTORNEY

- What do I need to do about probate?
- What do I do about his estate?
- How will the inheritance affect me?
- How will the inheritance affect my children?
- What do I need to do to protect myself and my children going forward?
- Do I need a new will?
- Do I need to set up a trust?
- What do I need to get done in the next month?
- What do I need to get done in the next year?

NOTES: _____

_____

_____

_____

_____

_____

_____

_____

_____

_____

_____

_____

_____

_____

_____

_____

_____

_____

_____

## A note on working with your attorney

In my experience, most attorneys do not want to hold your hand. So the more information you can bring to them organized in a way they can understand, the better. Most attorneys charge on an hourly basis. When you meet with an attorney, most of the time you want to go in with a business mind set. Keep the pleasantries short, sweet and to the point. The meter is still running, whether you get down to business or spend the first half-hour talking about how great your late husband was and the circumstances surrounding his death.

## A note on working with your tax professional

I have found that CPAs and other tax professionals are more than willing to help with all the tax-related aspects of sorting out finances after a death. I have seen their hearts go out to surviving spouses. In my opinion, there is much less risk of being taken advantage of by a tax professional, so you do not have to be as vigilant when making your choice or when working with them. The tax professional will also be able to help you construct a time line: what is important to get done in the next month, the next week, the next year.

## Chapter 3 Recap

- If you don't already have a team of trusted advisors in place, you need to assemble your team.
- From the recommendations you received, interview several candidates and take someone you trust with you to the interviews.
- Carefully evaluate the candidates. Look for someone who has extensive experience helping people in your situation, who is highly qualified, who listens well, and who can explain things clearly and seems willing to educate you.
- Avoid people who have a vested interest in selling you something, those who do not want you to bring someone with you to the interview, and those whose eagerness sends up a red flag.
- When choosing a financial advisor, consider how involved you want to be, or are able to be, in managing a financial plan.

- Unless you are experienced and comfortable with handling investments, and have the clarity of mind right now to deal with that, your best choice will probably be an asset-based-fee financial advisor who is also a Certified Financial Planner.

- After you've chosen your advisors and are ready to work with them, take someone you trust with you to the meetings. You may not be able to absorb everything the professional tells you, and this person can serve as your back-up memory and sounding board later.

- Take your list of questions with you to initial meetings, especially to meetings with your attorney, to make the best use of the professional's time.

- Using daily checklists and time lines can help you prioritize tasks and can give you a sense of accomplishment. It will also enable you to tackle issues one at time rather than trying to grapple with everything at once.

- Putting your issues, questions and relevant paperwork, as they come up, into a box for each advisor can relieve anxiety by allowing you to put things out of your mind until your meeting. And you won't have to worry about forgetting them.

### *In her own words*

*Oh, the paperwork! I'm not a person who likes doing financial stuff, so I thought, "Man, the last thing I want to do is spend hours dealing with all this." That's why I leaned heavily on Brad to get me through it. And what I needed was small doses, little bits and pieces, because otherwise it was too overwhelming. You need to know you've got someone you can count on who you're going to see every week. We met every Thursday, for a year or two. It was very comforting, almost like medication, because I knew, "Okay. I'm going to meet with him. I can deal with these questions then."*

*It would have been awful to have to struggle with that by myself. I probably would have said the money and the stock isn't that important to me, just because I hate dealing with it. I don't like doing the paperwork, but I'm glad that we did. I remember I'd come out of those meetings actually feeling uplifted, believe it or not. It would uplift me because I was doing something I needed to do. I was taking care of my business, bit by bit, whether it was figuring out how to pay a bill or closing out an account that I didn't need. Every time we met, we got something accomplished. And that felt good.*

## Chapter 4: The Important, But Not Urgent, Issues

Except for the urgent matters we covered earlier, most of the time just doing nothing—and doing nothing in haste—is the proper approach for the first six months to a year. After you have made some progress with processing your emotions and you have made some peace with your new situation, you can start to make plans for your future.

Some of the issues you may need to address are:

- Thinking about your long-range financial goals and income needs
- Your house and living situation
- Whether to go back to work
- Insurance
- Updating wills and trusts
- Planning for your children's education
- Disposition of a business
- What to do with vehicles
- Handling debt
- Remarrying eventually

These issues should not be considered separately, but should be evaluated by taking a holistic approach.

### Your long-range goals and income needs

You may not be able to think about this while you are grieving the loss of your spouse, but as soon as you are ready, it's important to start thinking about your goals and future income needs. You will have goals and needs encompassing many different aspects of your life: financial, physical, spiritual, family, and professional, to name some of them. These goals and income needs are going to dictate or influence the other major decisions you need to make. So as you are able to formulate them, write down your goals and income needs and share them with your advisors.

Some goals may be obvious to you. For example, if your children are nearing college age, you may want to make sure their college expenses are covered. You can make that a priority, and your advisors can help shape your plan to make it happen. Or if you do not want to go back to work, your advisors can put that into the plan. Now in some cases, they may have to come back and tell you there is not enough money to accomplish your goal. At that point, the goal or your priorities can change.

If you and your advisor team can prioritize your important decisions by keeping all of your goals and income needs in mind, taking an overall holistic approach to your financial planning, it will result in decisions you will be happier with over the long run.

Here's an example of a holistic approach. Suppose your goal is to pay off your house. But taking a holistic view and considering your future income needs, we discover that there isn't enough money to both pay off your house and allow you not to go back to work. Then we can ask, "Would you be willing to continue to make a house payment if it meant you didn't have to go back to work? Or would you be you happy to go back to work if it meant you can pay off your house? Or what if you went back to work, and continued to make a house payment and we could make this money supplement your income so you could put your kids through school?"

The specifics will vary with each person's situation. But if you can take a holistic approach, you are far less likely to discover too late that one isolated decision you made now made it impossible for you to achieve another important goal down the road.

> ᘒ *In her own words*
>
> *I think one thing that happens when people are suddenly single is they want the same lifestyle they had when they were married. They want to go places, they want to go to the stores and buy things and just whip out the credit card, when they don't have the income any more. So, you have to rethink your lifestyle. While you're dealing with a lot of grief, and your emotions are amped up high, you'll want to do things. I wanted to go out to eat. I wanted to buy things and do things that really I couldn't afford anymore.*

## A word about prioritizing you

In my practice, I have seen that some women have difficulty thinking about what they want and putting themselves first. They tend to be quite sensitive to the needs of other people around them and to put themselves last, and this tendency can affect their decision-making process. For example it can be hard to weigh, "Do I pay for the kids' college or do I fund my retirement?" It becomes a huge value decision that goes to the very heart of her identity. In reality it doesn't need to be all or nothing. It could be possible to help the kids out with college and put money towards retirement. But it may not feel that way to her.

If you are recently widowed, you need to spend time simply focusing on what you need and on taking care of yourself, even if you find it difficult. You may be thinking, "Oh I don't need a lot." But part of going through this process is looking at how much you need now and how much you will need for your future. If this is hard for you, you might benefit from some form of counseling or coaching, so that you can think about your future and your goals first, then gradually add back in and balance the needs of your family, friends, and others.

> ✑ *In her own words*
>
> *Don't be afraid to ask for help. Don't be afraid to tell people your situation. For instance, if you were at the hospital for weeks taking care of your spouse, it's possible to lose track of your finances and end up with hundreds of dollars of insufficient funds fees from your bank. You can go to the bank manager and explain what happened. There are a lot of people that are very sympathetic and could forgive a fee or a penalty. And don't be afraid to seek out other resources for yourself. I went to a grieving workshop and they gave us a lot of good information. There are many agencies that can help you move forward in whatever direction you need to go.*

## Your house

One of the most important decisions a widow typically faces is whether to stay in her house. It can feel like, "If I have a roof over my head, I'm in a great situation going forward." So it's important to look at the house in relation to the whole financial picture and financial plan for the future.

Your income needs are of paramount importance in making this decision. Once we establish your needs, we can determine your best housing situation. If your income needs are already fully met—meaning there is more than enough income from life insurance and/or investments to meet your needs going forward and you know that you're not going to have to go to work—you are in a good situation. You can stay where you are indefinitely.

However, many widows are not in that situation. For example, if we look at your financial resources and there is no income other than Social Security death benefits and IRA income, then your biggest asset is your house, or the equity in your house.

In that case, what are your options? If your children are grown, will one or more of them move back home and pay rent to help you stay in the house? Should you move out of the area to someplace less expensive? Are you going to try to make ends meet? Are you going to get roommates? Do you feel comfortable about that?

It may be that you have to make the decision at some point to sell your house to meet your future income needs. But as I said before, if you can put that decision off for as long as possible, at least until we have a complete picture of what your income situation will be, that will give you time to explore your options, to really think things through and to make the best decision.

## Should you go back to work?

Another important decision is whether to go back to work. Like many other widows, you may be in a situation where your husband was the breadwinner. You may not be sure you will have enough income to last, basically your whole life, now that his income is gone.

Inthatcase, your advisor will need to do a financial planto determine your present income needs, your retirement income needs, and the income that can be generated from your assets. An evaluation of these three factors will reveal whether you need to return to work.

## Insurance

Long-term health insurance for you and your minor children is another important issue. If you were eligible for COBRA, what will you do for health care coverage after it expires? With the help of your advisors, you will need to find a provider. If there are pre-existing conditions, those may affect your ability to obtain coverage as well as the cost of that coverage. The cost of health care must be factored into your future income needs.

In addition to health insurance, other insurance needs must be considered. Is your insurance coverage adequate to meet your current needs? And if you have children, will they receive adequate benefits if something happens to you?

## Updating wills and trusts

You will need to meet again with your attorney to make sure that your will and any trusts are updated appropriately for your current situation. You may have had estate planning in place with your spouse, and those plans may now need to change. You want to make sure your estate is in good order if you intend to pass it on to the next generation. And if you are among the sixty percent of Americans who do not have a will, by all means have one drawn up by your attorney.

## Planning for your children's education

If you have young children, you and your spouse may have put financial products in place, such asatrustor college-savings investment, to fund their higher education. If your name is not on those accounts, it can be a difficult and lengthy process to get the name changed. And it's something that must happen before you will be able to access those funds when they are needed.

If no provisions had been made for funding education, and if you want to contribute to the cost of higher education for your children, you need to determine how you will pay for it. Should you use the life insurance to fund college investments? Should you consider prepaid tuition? Your financial advisor can help you explore all your options.

## Disposition of a business

If your spouse owned a business, you will need to decide what to do with it. I have seen many widows whose spouses were business owners suddenly find themselves in charge of the business. If that is your situation, you will need to decide if you are going to keep the business or sell it. That's an important decision, but in most cases it doesn't need to be made in the first three to six months. In the meantime, you need to take the necessary steps to keep the business running.

Many times family members will take over a small business and keep it going. But if you and other family members have no experience in the business, and with the experienced person deceased, the business might not be as successful and therefore may not be worth as much as when that person was alive.

But a decision to sell too soon could be one you end up regretting. There can be serious tax repercussions from selling a business if all the income from the sale is taken in one year. Your tax professional and financial advisor will be able to help you explore other options, such as creating an installment payment contract to ease the tax liability.

## What to do with vehicles

Another decision you may be facing is what to do with vehicles. Once again, this is not an urgent matter. But the number of cars, trucks, motor homes, boats, and other vehicles that made sense for a couple might not make sense for you now as a single person. You may want to divest yourself of some of them to reduce the income drain from insurance, upkeep and storage. You will need to update the vehicle ownership and registration information, and you also need to update your insurance coverage so that there is only one person on the policies. In most cases you can take your time deciding which vehicles you want to keep. Like your other decisions, this one will be influenced by your holistic financial picture. If you need the income, that factor may outweigh the emotional value of some of the possessions, and you may decide to sell them.

## Consider an estate sale

If you are selling your house, downsizing or otherwise moving, a house full of belongings can be one more problem to deal with. There are your late spouse's clothes, tools, hobby or collection items, and more. There may be surplus linens, souvenirs and mementos, or sets of dishes that you really don't need. You will want to keep some things, of course. But do you want to pay to put furniture and other items in storage? Can you manage the cataloging and sale of the other stuff?

Many widows decide to have an estate sale and have a professional take over who works for a percentage of sale proceeds—typically about one-third. The professional will catalog, price, display and advertise everything you want to sell. He or she will donate to charity anything that doesn't sell and that you still don't want. You won't have to be on the premises; in fact, most professionals prefer that you not be. At the conclusion of the sale, you'll be provided with the proceeds and a complete accounting of all items sold. To find such professionals, consult the Internet or the phone book. There are usually several listed in every urban area. As with any person or service you hire, interview several and ask for references.

---

⌨ *In her own words*

*One of the hardest things for me to deal with was selling things. When I finally sold the house and had to get rid of the furniture because I was moving into my new husband's home, I felt a lot of emotional attachment. I've seen people rent storage units to hold on to stuff that, really, is just stuff. Maybe your husband had a collection of some kind and you don't have the heart to get rid of it. Let's say he had a coin collection, and you're renting a safe deposit box for $150 a year to store these coins you never even go look at. Somebody else could get a lot more joy out of it. Sell it. Boats, cars—sell them. Then you don't have to worry about storing and maintaining them.*

*Sometimes you're saving something for other people. "You know, this was your grandpa's best motorcycle and I'm going to give it to you," when maybe the kid could care less about a motorcycle, when you could take it and do something different with it. Donate it to your favorite charity, or sell it and give the money to your grandson instead. Sometimes people don't have the heart to tell you that they really don't want something.*

---

## Managing debt

Once you get your paperwork in order, if there is a substantial amount of debt—credit card debt, external loans, car loans, for example—you will need to decide whether you will make the minimum payments or pay off the debt with the life insurance policies.

There may also be real estate holdings that you are making payments on, such as time-shares, second homes or rental properties, and you will need to decide whether to continue carrying those loans or sell the properties or shares.

Once again, these decisions should be based solely on your present and future income needs. For example, if you have $1 million to invest, your financial advisor can give you a certain amount of income based on your risk tolerance. If that income is not enough to support the debt service, then you will need to eliminate the debt first.

If you have no debt as a widow, that is the best way to go through trying times. If you don't owe anything to anyone, you're in a much better position all around, and you have more options.

For an excellent book with a proven plan for eliminating debt and putting yourself on a solid financial footing, read *The Total Money Makeover* by Dave Ramsey. See the Resources chapter at the end of this book for details.

## Remarrying

One more topic that may be hard to think about, but which falls into the important-but-not-urgent category is whether you feel like you could ever remarry. Some people can never picture themselves being with someone else after a spouse passes away. Others eventually see it as an opportunity to go out and meet new people, and possibly someday get together with someone new. This is certainly not a decision that needs to be made today. But in your overall financial picture, it is important to consider, because you and your attorney may want to look at a prenuptial agreement if you ever did consider remarrying or getting involved in another intimate relationship.

---

*℘ **In her own words***

*You need to realize that when you lose your mate, you'll feel this unending emptiness. There is the loss of your mate and the loss of finances being brought in and it creates this massive void. And one way or another, even if you are seeing a therapist or taking medication for depression or anxiety, you will attempt to fill the void. I filled the void by spending money. Some women fill it with food. You need to be very careful how you're filling that void. You're better off filling it with love and work and with knowledge that will give you more power, instead of going out and spending your money on things to dull the emptiness.*

---

## Chapter 4 Recap

- After you've made some progress working through your emotions, you can start to address the important, but not urgent, issues and start to plan for your future.
- As soonas youare ready, it's important to start thinking aboutyour long-term goals and income needs, because they will influence many aspects of your financial plan and the decisions you will make.
- Take time to focus on your needs—what you need now and what you will need for your future—and make that a priority.
- With your advisors, take a holistic approach to your financial planning.
- Many important decisions, such as your living situation and whether to go back to work, will be largely determined by that holistic view and your future income needs.
- Accept adjustments you may have to make to your lifestyle.
- Don't be afraid to ask for help.
- If you applied for COBRA, you need to arrange for continuing health insurance coverage after COBRA.
- Meet with your attorney to update any wills and trust. Have your attorney draw up a will if you do not already have one.
- If you intend to contribute to the cost of higher education for your children, make plans for funding that if there is nothing already in place.
- If your spouse owned a business, decide if you want to keep it or sell it, and explore the tax ramifications of your options with your tax professional.
- Decide what vehicles to keep and update the titles, registration and insurance policies.
- Consider an estate sale to dispose of items you do not need, rather than paying storage, maintenance and insurance on items you won't use.
- Discuss with your financial advisor how to manage any debt.
- Although it may not be something you can think about right now, you may at some point want to remarry or become involved in an intimate relationship, and at that time you may want to discuss a prenuptial agreement with your attorney.

# Laurel's Story

After a short illness, Laurel's husband Richard succumbed to a secondary infection and died unexpectedly. Overnight he was gone. After thirty-five years of marriage and now in her late fifties, Laurel was suddenly on her own.

Richard was a wheeler-dealer and an aggressive, risk-taking investor. He had also been funding their affluent lifestyle largely through a home equity line of credit and credit cards. After he died, Laurel found, to her surprise, that with all of the credit card and home equity debt, they had very little money apart from the equity in their house. And because of the balance on the home equity line of credit, she didn't have nearly the amount of equity in the house that she thought she had. It was a rude awakening for her to realize how deeply they had gone into debt.

The credit cards were all virtually maxed out, and the total credit card debt was more than $70,000. The home equity line was also maxed out from large purchases. In addition they had two time-shares, neither one paid for, and debt service that needed to be paid every month on those. Richard had been making a good income, but without him, there was little or no money coming in. With the house payment and all the debt service payments, Laurel's monthly expenses were running about $16,000 a month.

We realized Laurel would probably need to sell the house, but I recommended that she try to wait six months before doing it. I also recommended we use the life insurance to pay down the credit cards. And I suggested we sell some of the possessions they had acquired to raise money to help pay off the credit cards. They had a boat, they had cars, they had tools—a lot of possessions.

Well, as you can imagine, trying to sell her husband's tools was emotionally wrenching for Laurel. At the same time, she was very angry at the financial position she had been left in, especially since she hadn't known about it. Richard and Laurel were living the lifestyle of someone making $300,000 a year. Now that income was gone, and Laurel's life had changed completely.

I felt the most urgent thing to do in Laurel's situation was to pay down those credit cards as quickly as possible and get rid of the debt. The hard part was convincing Laurel that debt was not a good thing. They had funded their lifestyle through debt, and it was a great lifestyle. It was taking trips. It was vacation homes. It was a 5,000-square-foot house. It was nice cars. It was all of these things—all on payments. They could afford the payments because of

Richard's salary. But once he passed away, she could not afford that lifestyle on a widow's Social Security benefits. She just could not afford the debt service.

Because some of the credit cards were in Richard's name only, we were able to get the credit card companies to forgive a portion of the debt. Even though she and Richard were married, Laurel's name was not on those cards. By going through her attorney and having him write a letter, we were able to save her about $25,000 that the credit card companies forgave.

Laurel is now trying to sell her house. In a depressed real estate market, she may realize only $200,000 on it after having lived there for twenty years, because the value of the house and therefore the equity in it has dropped. But Laurel no longer has a choice. It has been more than a year, and she realizes now that she has to sell the house. She also needs to get a job. As much as she might not want to, she sees that she must do both of those things. It has been a hard and slow realization for her. When Richard was alive, she thought they had a lot of money, but she learned that when it is all going to service debt, it's not much money at all.

After all is said and done, Laurel has about $250,000 to live on—for the rest of her life. When you think that she was used to spending $250,000 a year, you see why it's been a very difficult reality for her to face. Not only is she grieving for her husband, she's also angry with him for the debt that he left her and for leaving her with her situation in life altered forever.

I firmly believe that all widows should go through life with no debt. No credit card debt. No car debt. No debt. Period. Okay, maybe you can have a mortgage on your house. But think of Emma's situation: it freed her up when she had no house payment. Her life is very simple right now. She takes care of her kids, she makes sure they have as normal a life as possible, she takes a vacation once a year, and she volunteers in the community. I think that many widows would actually love to have Emma's life if they could. But that's not the reality. Laurel's situation is more the reality, one that dictates, "I've got to go back to work. I've got to sell my house. And I have a limited amount of money left to live on." That's a very difficult situation.

Richard and Laurel's story is a warning. Her reality has been altered, and she must radically downsize her life. But you take the hand that you are dealt in life, and you make the best of it, and that is what Laurel is trying to do now.

## Chapter 5: In Conclusion

Very little compares to losing a spouse; that long-term relationship is difficult to replace. It is a huge blow, one that you would not wish on anyone, but I would like to reassure you that you can survive it. You do have the resources, both inside yourself and outside, not only to make it through this experience but to emerge in good shape and live a good life in the future.

The unexpected death of my dad shaped me and drove me to become the person I am today. It also forced my mom to do things she never expected to have to do. Faced with this adversity, my mom and the many widows I have worked with found great strength within themselves and rose to the challenge that life presented. I believe that you can, too.

You have a lot of work ahead of you. But the individual steps required are small. If you just take it slowly, step by step, and put the most important tasks first, you will get through it all. When you are making decisions, remember to trust your heart and your instincts.

I would like to remind you, too, that you don't have to do it all alone. There are people who will help you. One of the main themes in the stories I have included is hope. Even when you think there is no hope, there will be people who will lift you up and help you figure out the next steps. And in a small way, I hope the information and basic themes of this book will help you get through the first few years, in the best possible way.

My wife Aimee asked me recently, "How often do you think of your dad?" He passed away over twenty years ago, yet my response was, "Every day." You may think about the spouse you lost every day for the rest of your life. But time really does heal. Through this amorphous, wonderful thing we call time, the pain will ease, and hopefully you will be left with wonderful memories to cherish as you move forward with your life.

---

*⌇ **In her own words***

*You will get better. I can assure you that you will feel better. It's not always going to be this way. It will be okay. It will be fine. For the sake of the loved one you've lost, remember the good times and don't let yourself stay sad forever. You have wonderful memories that no one can ever take away from you. Celebrate those wonderful memories that you have.*

---

# Natalie's Story

My client Natalie was getting older when she was diagnosed with breast cancer. She was undergoing treatment and was struggling with her health, when one day she got a call from her husband's boss telling her that Roy had been killed in an accident at work. She always thought she would be the first one to go. Then out of nowhere, her husband Roy died suddenly on the job. "No," she thought. "This wasn't supposed to happen."

Natalie's grieving process was especially difficult not only because she thought she would die first but also because she was dealing with serious health issues at the same time she was mourning his loss and trying to make a number of important financial decisions.

I have to hand it to Natalie for the way she dealt with the insurance companies. Because Roy's death was work-related, there would be workman's compensation in addition to life insurance. The insurance companies kept calling her every week to offer her money to compensate her for the death of her spouse. But in her heart she knew his life was worth more than what the insurance companies were offering.

So she did some research, talked to me, talked to a couple of attorneys and realized that she could get a settlement from the insurance company that was much more than what they were offering. The insurance companies assumed Natalie would jump at their offers because she was a widow with few financial resources who they assumed needed the money. So Natalie just waited. Waited. Waited them out. She ultimately received nearly the full amount she thought she should get, based on the insurance levels and the worker's compensation. Had she not waited, had she just taken the first offers, she would not be in the position she is now financially where she can live her life, go on vacation if she wants, treat herself well, and focus on her health.

When we first talked, Natalie thought she might want to buy a house with the insurance money. I asked her why, in her late sixties, she would want to become a homeowner. She told me it was something she had always wanted to accomplish. But just by postponing the decision and exploring her options over time, she was able to decide that home ownership might not be the way she wanted to spend the next fifteen or so years of her life.

In the end, we decided to invest the money and create an income stream that she felt good about and one that would allow her to quit her job. She was able to retire with this money and go forward from there. During the course of her marriage, Natalie had relied on her husband to make most of the financial decisions. But Roy was something of a spender, and most of the money they had earned over the course of their working lives was gone.

After Roy passed away, Natalie educated herself wisely, analyzed her options, and moved forward well from there. I give her credit for waiting out the settlement with the insurance companies and for waiting to decide whether to buy a house or take the income. This decision was made over the course of a year or two. And it allowed her to keep everything status quo for a while, just paying her bills, keeping her job, and continuing her treatments. She didn't do anything rash. And she was able to let time help her make good decisions.

# Helpful Resources

**Website articles**

*How to Choose a Financial Advisor,* a comprehensive article on the Wall Street Journal website (www.online.wsj.com). guides.wsj.com/personal-finance/.../how-to-choose-a-financial-planner/

*Investment Advisors: What You Need to Know About Choosing One,* another good article on the U.S. Securities and Exchange Commission website (www.sec.gov). See especially the section "How do Investment Advisors Get Paid?" The full url is: http://www.sec.gov/investor/pubs/invadvisers.htm

*How to Choose a Planner,* 10 Questions to Ask When Choosing a Financial Planner publications.usa.gov/epublications/financial-planner/10questions.html.

*The Five Stages of Grief,* a summary of the stages of the grieving process and suggestions for those who suddenly become single parents. This article is on the mental-health-matters.com website and was written by Single Parent Central, www.singleparentcentral.com. Single Parent Central offers information and resources to single-parent families.

**Resource for young widows**

YoungWidow.org is a website that is exclusively dedicated to young widows and widowers. It is sponsored by Young Widow - Chapter Two, a nonprofit corporation.

## Books

*The 7 Habits of Highly Effective People* by Steven Covey, published by Free Press in 1989, contains more information on prioritizing important versus urgent issues. Available from most bookstores, amazon.com, and stevencovey.com.

I recommend Dave Ramsey's books, particularly *The Total Money Makeover* which describes a proven plan for managing and eliminating debt and putting yourself on a solid financial footing. Published by Thomas Nelson, 2003 and 2007.

Elizabeth Kubler-Ross's classic book, *On Death & Dying* is a complete presentation of the five stages of grief. Originally written about people facing their own death, the stages have been considered to apply to the survivors of the death of a loved one as well. Published by Simon & Schuster/Touchstone, 1969.

## Contact Brad

Brad Ledwith
Ledwith Financial Wealth Management
55 West 1st Street
Morgan Hill, CA 95037
408-778-3000
brad@ledwithfinancial.com
www.ledwithfinancial.com

# ADDITIONAL NOTES

# ADDITIONAL NOTES

# ADDITIONAL NOTES

# ADDITIONAL NOTES

# ADDITIONAL NOTES

# ADDITIONAL NOTES

# Acknowledgements

*I would like to thank the following people whose help was invaluable to me in writing this book: my wife Aimee, my mom Cindy, Kathy, Jim, Marti, Bill, Bob, Debbi, Maureen, KOC, Ryan A, Renee, Pam, Del, Kim and Shellie*